Evening
PRAYERS

Publications International, Ltd.

$\mathcal{A}$t the end of the day, it is good to turn our hearts, our thoughts, and our prayers to God. Whether the day included successes or defeats, whether it was a day where we were aware of God's blessings or one where we were too rushed to appreciate God's presence, setting some time aside in the evening allows us to reflect on the joys and sorrows of the day. It gives us the opportunity to ask for forgiveness and to offer thanks and praise. It gives us peace of mind and heart.

In peace I will lie down and sleep,

for you alone, Lord,

make me dwell in safety.

Psalm 4:8, NIV

Blessings for This Night

The day has been long, Lord, but that's water under the bridge. Bless me now with stillness, sleep, and restful dreams. I sigh and turn over, knowing that night will usher in the day with new joys and possibilities, gifts from your ever-wakeful spirit.

SOUND SLEEPERS

Security, loving God, is going to sleep in the assurance that you know our hearts before we speak and are waiting, as soon as you hear from us, to transform our concerns into hope and action, our loneliness into companionship, and our despair into dance.

O Love of God, descend into my heart;

Enlighten the dark corners of this neglected dwelling,

And scatter there Your cheerful beams.

Dwell in the soul that longs to be Your temple;

Water that barren soil overrun with weeds and briars

And lost for lack of cultivating.

Make it fruitful with Your dew.

Come, dear Refreshment of those who languish;

come, Star and Guide of those who sail amidst tempests.

You are Haven of the tossed and shipwrecked.

Come now, Glory and Crown of the living,

As well as the Safeguard of the dying.

Come, Sacred Spirit;

Come, and make me fit to receive You.

Saint Augustine

Reading
Your Word

Lord, speak to me through these pages.
Let me hear your gentle words
come whispering through the ages
and thundering through the world.

Challenge me and change me,
comfort me and calm me.
Completely rearrange me,
soothe me with a psalm.

Teach me how to please you,
show me how to live.
Inspire me to praise you
for all the love you give.

A PRAYER FOR RESTORATION

Calm me enough, O Lord, to breathe deeply
and restoratively despite my racing heart,
pounding headache, and generally fatigued
body and mind. Prayer restores me in the
presence of all that threatens to undo me,
which I name to you now.

Star Signs

To those scanning a night sky, you sent a star. To those tending sheep on a silent hill, you sent a voice. What sign, Lord, are you sending me to come, be, and do all you intend? Let me hear, see, and accept it when you do.

Trusting in Spite of Trouble

Dear Lord, each night the news is full of trouble. So much pain and sorrow. It makes me ache to see it all. Some nights, it seems that's all there is; this world seems sometimes so weary and heavy laden. Then I turn to you and know that you are nearest on the darkest days. And there is comfort in knowing you and that you have not forsaken us or the people whose world is presently dark. Amen.

And they that know thy name will put their trust in thee: for thou, Lord, hast not forsaken them that seek thee.

Psalm 9:10

Rest in the Lord

When the nights seem long, the days feel like a struggle, and the spirit is weary, we find a resting place in God's enduring love, and we know that his plan for us is good. This is the true meaning of letting go and letting God's higher will be done in our lives.

You have made us for yourself and our hearts are restless until they rest in you.

St. Augustine

Under His Wings

Under his wings I am safely abiding,
though the night deepens and tempests are wild;
still I can trust him, I know he
will keep me,
he has redeemed me and I am his child.
Under his wings, under his wings,
who from his love can sever?
Under his wings my soul shall abide,
safely abide forever.
Under his wings, O what precious enjoyment!
There will I hide till life's trials are o'er;
sheltered, protected,
no evil can harm me,
resting in Jesus I'm safe evermore.
Under his wings, under his wings,
who from his love can sever?
Under his wings my soul shall abide,
safely abide forever.

William O. Cushing

In Thanksgiving for Healing

*C*reator God, you have come to me with healing in your hand. When I cried out, you heard me. You provided me with a gift that brought both peace and pleasure to my harried life. You helped me to focus on life instead of illness and sorrow. Lord, thank you for this wondrous gift. Amen.

SHEEP OF GOD'S PASTURE

Despite today's valley of shadow and sickness, I know you, shepherd of my soul, will continue restoring me as I move through treatment to the safe meadow of wellness.

Reflecting on Forgiveness

Forgiveness is the central virtue in God's treasure chest—God's forgiveness of us and our forgiveness of others and ourselves. At times we find that forgiveness comes very easily, even for grievous and painful hurts. But many times, we seem powerless to forgive, no matter how hard we try. This is when God's forgiving grace has the opportunity to touch and change us and then be extended to others through our example.

Dear God, as I reflect on my day, I thank you for your forgiveness for my failings and faults. I ask you to help me to forgive those who have hurt me today or in the past. Amen.

A Heart of Forgiveness

Lord, I need you to help me with the concept of forgiving people over and over again for the same behavior. I know you taught that there was no limit to the number of times we should forgive someone, but I get so weary of doing it, Lord. Help me to have a heart of forgiveness, so ready to forgive that I do so before the person who has wronged me even seeks my forgiveness. There's freedom in that kind of forgiveness, Lord. Help me claim it for my own.

Amen.

And when ye stand praying, forgive, if ye have ought against any: that your Father also which is in heaven may forgive you your trespasses.

Mark 11:25

Pulled Apart

*L*ord, what a day it was. Like a turkey wishbone, God of wholeness, I am being pulled apart by job, family, home, errands, friends, and my needs. I'm preoccupied with what I didn't get done today and feel the pull to do it all. Help me choose wisely tomorrow and in the days to come. Remind me to negotiate on the job and at home for the time I need in both places. Remind me, O God, to negotiate for a leaner lifestyle, for I am part of the pull. In the tugging days ahead, be the hinge that keeps my life's parts synchronized in harmonious movement, not split apart at all.

Reflections of Light

Held up to your light, our broken hearts can become prisms that scatter micro-rainbows on the wall. Our pain is useless as it is, redeeming God, just as a prism is a useless chunk of glass until light passes through it. Remind me that the smallest ray of sun in a shower can create a rainbow. Use my tears as the showers and your love as the sun. Looking up, I see the tinest arches of hope in the lightening sky.

> They that sow in tears shall reap in joy.
> He that goeth forth and weepeth, bearing
> precious seed, shall doubtless come again
> with rejoicing, bringing his sheaves with him.
>
> Psalm 126:5–6

For Our Family

May your eyes look kindly upon this family, Lord, tonight and always, for we need your love and guidance in our lives. This is a family that seeks to do the right things—to work hard for a living, to raise up children who will contribute to society, and to be a blessing in our neighborhood. But we know we need your constant help to do these things. May we be filled with love and happiness—all of us who live in this home—by fulfilling our responsibilities, day in and day out; by being accountable in all our actions; by giving whenever we can, even when it hurts; by nurturing warmth and understanding among us. Let us always look out for the best interests of others. Please grant our requests according to your great goodness.

Remembering Family

Keep us connected, O God of all time, to those who've come before. Inspire us to tell family tales and to pull out family albums and family Bibles and handed-down antiques to show the connecting links from which your love forges us into a whole.

For he that is mighty hath done to me great things; and holy is his name. And his mercy is on them that fear him from generation to generation.

Luke 1:49–50

An Abundance of Angels

Lord, I know that you simply cannot be everywhere at once, so you made angels to help you spread your loving grace upon the earth. Thank you for blessing my life with an abundance of angels in the form of friends and family members who love and care for me. They fill my life with joy and give me wings to follow my dreams.

FOR THOSE THAT WELCOME

Lord, how grateful I am for the gift of hospitality. When others make me feel welcome in their home, it fills me with warmth and love. Help me to cultivate this gift in myself, Lord, so that those who enter my home may find sweet joy and hope.

May He support us all the day long, till the shades lengthen, and the evening comes, and the busy world is hushed, and the fever of life is over, and our work is done! Then in His mercy may He give us a safe lodging, and a holy rest, and peace at the last.

John Henry Newman

$\mathcal{I}$ will lift up mine eyes unto the hills, from whence cometh my help.

My help cometh from the Lord, which made heaven and earth.

He will not suffer thy foot to be moved: he that keepeth thee will not slumber.

Behold, he that keepeth Israel shall neither slumber nor sleep.

Psalm 121:1–4

A Prayer
of Confession

Lord God, I kneel before you, and you alone.

I'm sorry for the times I've mistakenly

Credited someone else or something else

For your miraculous work.

How could an angel, a preacher, a friend

Impart your healing power, unless

You were behind it all,

Inspiring, instructing, empowering?

I thank you for the ones you use

On this earth and in your heaven

To help me heal.

Lord God, I kneel before you, and you alone.

Amen.

At Night

O Lord God, who has given us the night for rest, I pray that in my sleep my soul may remain awake to you, steadfastly adhering to your love. As I lay aside my cares to relax and relieve my mind, may I not forget your infinite and unresting care for me. And in this way, let my conscience be at peace, so that when I rise tomorrow, I am refreshed in body, mind and soul.

John Calvin

When thou liest down, thou shalt not be afraid: yea, thou shalt lie down, and thy sleep shall be sweet.

Proverbs 3:24

Waiting

So here I am, waiting. I have answered your call to pray. I have heard your guidance—to sit tight. I have chosen quiet and rest because that is your will for me now. I am sitting on the sidelines, watching the hectic pace around me. I am finding contentment in the little blessings that flow into my days. I am trying to see all these things as big blessings because they come from you. But when can I get going again? When will I do the great works I've envisioned? When will the situation require dedicated action once again? When will I hear the trumpet call? When will I finally move onward and upward? I'm ready, Great Spirit! Here I am…waiting.

I Did It!

O Lord, I savor this triumph: Today I met my goal! Day by day, I reached into my heart and found energy to keep on. Day by day, I reached out and found your hand leading, your inspiration guiding. Stand with me to celebrate our joint success.

IN THANKS FOR A GOOD DAY

How fortunate I feel today! All is well. Things are working out. But is it luck…or is it your love? I will assume the latter and offer words of praise: Bless your name, Almighty One!

Healing for the Mentally Ill

Mental illness can be so devastating, Lord. Few understand the heartaches involved in diseases that carry no apparent physical scars. Be with those friends, neighbors, and family members who deal daily with difficult situations of which we are often unaware. Touch them with your special love, and let them know that they can lean on you, Lord. Ease their burdens, quell their sadness, and calm their desperation. Bring peace and healing to these households tonight and all nights.

For thou hast been a strength to the poor, a strength to the needy in his distress, a refuge from the storm, a shadow from the heat.

Isaiah 25:4

A Prayer for Caretakers

$\mathcal{O}$ Lord, I know you take notice of them—the caretakers for the aged and the ill. They work selflessly for the most vulnerable among us, yet their efforts are so often overlooked. May they sense your presence beside them, Lord. May they feel your strength lifting them up and helping them through the most trying moments. Give them encouragement by helping them see what a difference they make in their patients' lives.

Pure religion and undefiled before God and the Father is this, To visit the fatherless and widows in their affliction, and to keep himself unspotted from the world.

James 1:27

A Grateful Prayer for Helpers

Lord, you've given me a great team of helpers,
And I'm exceedingly thankful.
Where would I have been today without them?
They seemed to know my needs before I did,
And they jumped to meet them.
I know you've given them those gifts of caring,
Of encouragement, of hospitality and healing,
But they're using those gifts as you intended,
To show your love to others—I mean me.
I am thankful to you and to them.
There's not much I can do to pay them back, Lord.
They'd probably refuse a reward anyway.
So I ask you to shower them with blessings,
Just as they have brought blessing to me.
Give them joy and peace in rich supply,
And let your love continue to flow
To them, within them, and through them.
Amen.

In Praise

Lord, if I were to boil down all the good news in the universe and look to see what I'd ended up with, there would be the eternal realities of your goodness, your love, and your faithfulness. And in this world, I don't have to look far for them—family, food, shelter, clothing, seasons, tides, sun, moon, stars, life, beauty, truth, salvation. And that's just a sampling, a preview of a much longer list. As I reflect on your awe-inspiring goodness tonight, I'm moved to praise you and to tell you how much I love you back.

So Little Time

Square by square, we live our lives marked off in neat appointment-calendar blocks of time. Everybody gets only so much, no more, for the lines are already bulging. We pencil in commitments that spill over into tomorrow's squares. And just look at yesterday's notations: Nowhere did we get every "to do" done, every deadline met. There is not enough time in the little squares we have allotted ourselves, O God, calling them life. We try using a larger calendar with bigger squares, but all we do is make our schedule heavier. Our pencils eat up our best intentions for accepting your promised abundant life. Help us, for we want to be more than just the sum of all we had scheduled, minus what we got done, multiplied by what we wished we'd been doing, tallying up to a bottom line of regret. Guide us as we erase what is not essential. Forgive us for the day-squares where we've inched you out; their hectic dreariness reflects your absence.

From Parent to Parent

*T*oday I lost patience with my child. Please help me never to do it again, God. Teach me to see myself just as you see me: a learner still discovering life's wisdom, still experimenting with right and wrong, still making foolish mistakes. And help me to be understanding with my child just as you have always been with me, all down through the years.

Ye have received the Spirit of adoption, whereby we cry, Abba, Father. The Spirit itself beareth witness with our spirit, that we are the children of God.

Romans 8:15–16

In Need of a Night-Light

*R*each out to me, a child again, lost, frightened, and alone with few answers for comfort. Stay with me until I fall asleep and be here if I awake scared. Let me be a child tonight, Lord. Tomorrow I'll be big and strong and all grown up, but for now, find me, hold me.

GIVING GOD CONTROL

Even if my motives are pure, O God, I need to step back and let you guide—all of us—instead of trying to control. Often my mouth is open before I think. Keep me quiet for the sake of peace and learning.

NO WAITING

Will tomorrow be less hectic and more inclined toward joy? Will I be less tired? I don't want to wait to find out. In your creation, joy can be found anytime, but mostly now. Keep reminding me that now is all of life I can hold at any moment. It cannot be banked, invested, hoarded, or saved. It can only be spent.

Trust in Busy Times

It's late at night, and still there is much to do. Yet there is peace, holding onto childlike trust that God is an ever-present companion, showing us how not to burn out needlessly, worrying the candle at both ends.

For Everyone in Times of Trouble

O Lord, hear my prayer for all who go to bed discouraged and sorrowful this night.

Comfort those who are facing the loss of a loved one. After the wrenching grief, let their lonely hours be filled with fond memories of days gone by.

Be with those who passed this day without work. During this time of financial stress, give them energy to make their employment the job of finding new work.

Encourage those who are finding it difficult to believe in the future. Let your hope fill their hearts as they recall all your past faithfulness.

Enlighten those doubting the truth of your existence or the validity of your promises. Bring wise friends into their lives who have long known the reality of your love.

Reassure those struggling to make ends meet. Let them be assured that you can take care of every need, no matter how large or small.

Heal those who are suffering pain and illness. Let them find rest and calm as they seek to make the idle moments pass more quickly.

Soothe those racked in mind and stressed out emotionally. Cradle their minds in your love and soothe every irrational thought that seeks to run out of control.

Uphold those who are being tempted in any way today, especially those who may want to end their lives. May they find joy in just one moment at a time. And may that be enough for now.

In all these ways I ask your blessing upon those in trouble. And please include me in that blessing, too! Amen.

Out of Steam

Looking back over my workday, it's clear that I have lost some of my zeal to do that work, God. Forgive me for falling into despair and for being on the lookout for a greener pasture at the expense of full concentration on the tasks at hand. Help me not to cheat my employer by only giving a half-hearted effort.

But most of all, I want to keep my eyes on you, Lord, not on things or places or the myriad circumstances beyond my control. I know that true happiness and fulfillment will come only from being in your will.

And when it is time to move, you will show me. Therefore, strengthen my faith in your goodness. For I know your commitment to me has never been in question. Your zeal for my life never cools. Praise you!

In Times of Struggle

God of the strong and the weak, the brave and the fearful, I come before you to place myself in your loving hands. Take my broken places and make them whole. Heal my wounds that I might be strong for you. Give me patience to accept your timing, and help me to trust in your goodness. In your gracious name, I pray. Amen.

The foolishness of God is wiser than men; and the weakness of God is stronger than men.

1 Corinthians 1:25

Trying to Trust

*O*ear God, waiting for you is the hardest part of life. Not knowing. Not understanding. Not being able to figure things out. And when you don't provide answers right away, I feel as if I'll go crazy. But when I stop a moment and think about it, it makes sense that there will be times when you ask me to just trust you, when you'll challenge my rhetoric about believing in you and teach me to be patient. So here I am. I'll be still and wait for you.

In thee, O Lord, do I put my trust; let me never be ashamed: deliver me in thy righteousness.

Psalm 31:1

Take My Life and Let It Be

Take my life, and let it be

consecrated, Lord, to thee;

take my moments and my days;

let them flow in ceaseless praise.

Take my hands, and let them move

at the impulse of thy love.

Take my feet, and let them be

swift and beautiful for thee.

Take my love, my Lord, I pour

at thy feet its treasure store.

Take myself, and I will be

ever, only, all for thee.

Frances Ridley Havergal

When I think about your faithfulness to me, Lord, my heart overflows! I long to share this treasure trove with the people around me. When I consider all that you have done for me, I am overwhelmed by your love.

There are many aspects of life that are easy to take for granted: the air that I breathe, the rain for the crops, the food that I eat, and the relationships that I have. I sometimes forget how blessed I am. I want to take time every day to really contemplate how faithfully you work in my life. Once all of your blessings are fresh in my mind, it will be impossible to hide my gratitude. Your faithfulness will be on the tip of my tongue and in the innermost recesses of my heart.

Laying Our Burdens Down

O God, I know you will never give us a burden to bear without giving us the grace to endure it, but some burdens just seem so heavy we find ourselves wondering if they can be survived. I ask that you send an abundant amount of strength and grace to all those who suffer so. Let them feel your presence in a very real way, Lord, for without you, they have no hope. I ask this in Jesus' name. Amen.

Loving Others

Lord above, you look down upon us, and still you love us. When we look down on others, it is because we are angered and cannot see their points of view. We also still love them, but sometimes our anger clouds our love. Please help us stay grounded and find understanding. Amen.

The patient in spirit is better than the proud in spirit. Be not hasty in thy spirit to be angry: for anger resteth in the bosom of fools.

Ecclesiastes 7:8–9

Renewal

Dear Lord, I need renewal in my life.
But tell me what you want me to be, first,
then tell me what you want me to do.
Speak, for I am listening,
Guide, for I am willing to follow.
Be silent, for I am willing to rest in your love.

Whate'er my fears or foes suggest,

Thou are my hope, my joy, my rest;

My heart shall feel thy love, and raise

my cheerful voice to sing of praise.

Isaac Watts

A Family Prayer

Dear God, for our family we ask your love and care in the days and years ahead. We pray for the strength to go to work every day. It's not easy to get up early and then go out to face the world. The competition is tough, the bottom line inflexible. Give us the strength to work.

We pray for the health of each family member. You know our bodies better than we do. Every ache and pain, every sickness, is a concern to you. Therefore we ask that you keep watch over our bones and muscles and every bodily system, because you are the Great Healer. We ask for guidance in all the decisions we must make in the days ahead, the big decisions, and even the little daily ones. We acknowledge that without divine direction, our lives become meaningless, wrapped up in our own selfishness, heading nowhere. Lead us where you want us to go!

Let us be friends with our neighbors. Especially give us patience when it seems our comforts are ignored or our rights infringed. In every dispute, let us be willing to be fair, and even take less than we deserve. And give us a spirit of humility that we might offer help and comfort when we see a neighbor in need.

For the students in this family, we pray for extended hours of concentration. We ask that the days of books and classes might be filled with energy and the joy of learning as you provide wisdom and intelligence. Give us time to play together, to have fun, to laugh. For we know that your dwelling place is a place of joy and laugher. Let us experience in this family a little bit of heaven on earth.

Finally, increase the strength of our bonds of love so that we might bear witness to your love in our community. Give us the desire to offer hospitality at every opportunity. And throughout all our days together, may this family learn to worship better and better, seeing all you have so graciously given us.

Amen.

On Insecurity

Lord, sometimes I long to stand out. I notice others with shinier hair, amazing figures, and impeccable outfits, and I feel so plain. At these times, help me to remember that I should be at work cultivating the gentle and quiet spirit that is precious to you. This type of spirit may not call out, "Here I am!" but over the long run, it accomplishes much. I am doing what I can, and I leave the rest to you. I trust that you will bring all to fruition.

> But the wisdom that is from above is first pure, then peaceable, gentle, and easy to be intreated, full of mercy and good fruits, without partiality, and without hypocrisy.
>
> James 3:17

An Offering of Praise

*Lord, no matter what we bring of ourselves
to give you, even if we include all our hopes
and dreams, it's never enough to give in
return for all you've given to us. And so
we give you our praise. We sing to you
and come before you with our meager
offerings, praying all the while that you
will make something marvelous of them.*

*B*y him therefore let us offer the sacrifice of
praise to God continually, that is, the fruit of our
lips giving thanks to his name.

Hebrews 13:15

Understanding Forgiveness

God,

You said we should, "Forgive us our sins as we forgive those who sin against us."

Do you realize how hard that can be?

When I've been hurt, my anger and resentment feels justified.

Yet I know that my lack of forgiveness hurts me as much as it hurts the one who hurt me.

I need your help with forgiveness.

Help me forgive anyone who has ever wounded me, however slight or great the hurt.

Forgive me both the offenses I did on purpose and the ways I hurt others without realizing it.

Whenever possible, let me know how to make amends to those I have hurt.

Help me accept forgiveness from others and graciously offer my own forgiveness. From now on, guide me in a way of living that respects other people and seeks to understand rather than to condemn their actions.

For this is the way that leads to life. Amen.

Priorities

Prioritizing spiritual realities over temporal ones is not always easy. The physical realities are tangible. I can hold a stack of bills in my hand and know that if I don't pay them, problems will arise. But those spiritual realities…well, the benefits (and consequences) are not always so easy to recognize or see in the moment. This is a faith issue, pure and simple. First, I need to stay calm about issues of provision. Second, I need to keep drawing near to you. Third, I need to reach out to others with your love. And after all of these things are done, I need to trust you with the results.

Your Word

father God, after a difficult day, when I face the temptation to give up on a task or a ministry opportunity, it helps to read about Abraham, Moses, Joseph, David, Job—all those whose times of trial and perseverance are so beautifully preserved for us through your Word. Once we become attuned to your plan for our lives, we can continue on with the certainty that you always complete what you start. We can stand firmly on your promises, confident that you will give us the strength we need to keep going. Thank you for the faith of the ages, Lord! It is also the faith for today.

Shining a Light

Lord, I admit that my light often shines more brightly outside the walls of my home than inside, and today was one of those days. The truth is that my family members—the ones dearest to me in the world—are usually the first ones to hear my murmuring and arguing and to see my "blemishes." And to add insult to injury, they're often the last ones to hear my confessions and apologies. There are plenty of excuses I could make about being around them more, having to deal with their "blemishes," and about needing to "be me" at home.

I want to be consistent in my walk with you, though. Tomorrow and always, give me the fortitude to shine my light first at home and then into the world around me.

In Thanks for Family

Lord, what compassion you showered on your people when you grouped us into families! Thank you, Lord, for the homes we are privileged to enjoy. We are thankful for these sanctuaries for our children and grandchildren. May our homes and our families honor you, Lord, in all we say and do within them. Dwell with us, Lord. You are always welcome. Amen.

Train up a child in the way he should go: and when he is old, he will not depart from it.

Proverbs 22:6

White Lies

Lord, today a little white lie slipped out of my mouth to save me from a trying commitment. As soon as I felt your little tug on my conscience, I knew I had to come clean about it and repair my relationship with you and with my friend. I know that the lie wasn't small in your eyes, and it was a reminder to me that I am always vulnerable to sin. If I didn't feel your nudge to repair the situation as quickly as possible, I might have fallen into a complacency that would make me vulnerable to any number of more serious sins. I thank you for nudging me, Lord, and for forgiving me, yet again.

Growing in Truth

I do sometimes prefer frivolity and flattery to growing in the light of some uncomfortable truth, Lord. You can see where I'm prone to skirting the issues I need to deal with, and you know when I'm indulging in foolishness when I could be having a meaningful interaction with someone who walks in the truth. I know it's okay to have fun, but it's good for me to look in the mirror regularly as well. Grant me the grace to soak in the wisdom that will change me for the better.

Seeking Your Peace

Lord, it's wearying trying to be on the cutting edge, working to "be somebody," scrambling to get to the top of the mountain first. Sometimes I need to pull away from the rat race and be quiet; to put away my goals, appointments, and lists and just be with you, Lord. I crave the peace of your presence, and I need to feel held by you. Please pick me up and let me lean against your heart, which I know is full of love for me and all the world.

Stand in awe, and sin not: commune with your own heart upon your bed, and be still.

Psalm 4:4

Being Known

Lord, what comfort I find in the knowledge that you know everything I've ever done. I know going over my sins with you is still necessary for my growth and development, but it helps to know I'll never have to hear you say, "I can't believe you did that!" You know my strengths and my weaknesses. You know my joy and my shame. And yet you still forgive me and have hope for me. Thank you, Lord, for caring enough to truly know me—and for loving me anyway.

Search me, God, and know my heart;
test me and know my anxious thoughts.
See if there is any offensive way in me,
and lead me in the way everlasting.

Psalm 139:23–24, NIV

Come, Holy Spirit

Jesus, your purposes are eternal ones, and they're generally the opposite of an earthbound here-and-now mind-set. Your Word makes it clear to me that it takes a committed heart and soul to follow you. So where I have become dusty or rusty in my attentiveness in following you, please come with the breath of your Spirit to refresh me and get me moving in your ways again.

But the Comforter, which is the Holy Ghost,

whom the Father will send in my name,

he shall teach you all things, and bring

all things to your remembrance,

whatsoever I have said unto you.

John 14:26

Your Love

Lord Jesus, the dimensions of your love are hard for me to comprehend because there is no other love like yours. No human love can compare with how deeply and thoroughly you love me. But just trusting that there is such a love as yours is the perfect beginning point for an adventure where I become delightfully lost in its immensity.

THE TRUE EXCITEMENT

When I'm bored, remind me:
This is the excitement of life—
darkness alternating with light,
down dancing with up,
and inactivity being absolutely essential
—as prelude—
to the most fulfilling experiences of all.

Thanksgiving for Your Promises

When you say something, Lord God, it is as good as done. It may not take place in the timing that I'd imagine or wish, but you are true to your word without fail. So when you tell me not to be anxious—but rather to pray and you will give me your peace—I'll just do that. When you say that you forgive me when I confess my sin, I'll believe that. When you tell me that I'm your child and that you rejoice over me, I'll take pleasure in that. Whatever you say, I'll not doubt it. Thank you for your great and precious promises and for your absolute trustworthiness. Amen.

A PRAYER OF PRAISE

Almighty God, we want to end this day by

praising you. Do we tell you often enough

how awesome you are? We stand before

you in complete awe of your creation, your

sovereignty, and your power. Let us never

minimize the ability you have to change our

reality in an instant, even when it involves

moving mountains or calming storms.

You, O God, are the one and only God,

and we give you glory at all times.

Your Truth

Truth is a narrow road, and it's easy to fall to one side or the other. For every beautiful kernel of truth, there are a thousand lies that can surround it. Staying on the straight-and-narrow would be impossible if it weren't for the Spirit of God, who leads us to all truth. Delving into God's Word with the Holy Spirit to guide us is the best way to stay on track and keep walking in the truth. O Holy Spirit, as I read your Word tonight, please open my heart to your truth.

And take the helmet of salvation, and the sword of the Spirit, which is the word of God.

Ephesians 6:17

Reflection

Lord, please forgive us in our impatient moments and nudge us back onto the right path. We live in a society that knows nothing of delayed gratification; we often get caught up in the expectation that everything we need from you and ask of you will happen immediately. But we know from experience that your timing is always perfect, Lord. We are blessed and privileged to have time for reflection and growth.

My beloved brethren, let every man be swift to hear, slow to speak, slow to wrath.

James 1:19

Answering the Call

Work was good today, God of all labor, and I think I know why: You and I were working together. Is this what it is to be called?

I think it must be, for you are the source of my talents, for which I am grateful. Through the support of others, gifted teacher, mentors, and leaders, and through those willing to take a chance on me despite the odds, you have always been present, and I am grateful for that, too.

Although this sense that I am doing what you intend for me is usually just a delicious, split-second awareness, O God, it is enough to keep me going when I am tired, frustrated, and unclear about my next step. Our companionship of call to vocation is not an instant process, but rather a shared journey. Keep me listening, watching.

I am glad we share this working venture, for on the job and off, I am blessed.

Prayer for a Friend

Lord, I know my friend is overwhelmed right now. Just as you lift my burdens when I come to you in prayer, show me what I can do to make her load lighter. I lay her troubles before you, Lord. I know our efforts can lift her burdens.

A friend loveth at all times, and a brother is born for adversity.

Proverbs 17:17

Abide with Me

Abide with me,
Fast falls the eventide;
The darkness deepens;
Lord, with me abide!
When other helpers fail
And comforts flee,
Help of the helpless,
O abide with me.
I need thy presence
Every passing hour;
What but thy grace
Can foil the tempter's power?
Who like thyself,
My guide and stay can be?
Through cloud and sunshine,
Lord, abide, with me.

Henry F. Lyte

Reflecting on Your Love

For years I was afraid to approach you—afraid you'd disapprove of me or declare me "unacceptable." When I finally sought you, I discovered you were tender, compassionate, loving. Now instead of fear, during my life's purest moments, I feel secure, embraced, totally accepted—and completely loved by you.

ASKING FOR HEALING

Heavenly Father, when I was young, I thought all things hurt or broken could be fixed: knees, feelings, bicycles, tea sets. Now I've learned that not everything can be repaired, relieved, or cured. As a mother comforts her child, heal my hurting and grant me the peace I used to know. This I pray.

Amen.

Meditating on Your Word

*Y*our Word really does cut to the heart of the matter when it comes to what life is about, Lord. It doesn't let me hide behind excuses, pretenses, or lies. It gives me the straight scoop without any meaningless frills. That kind of honesty is hard to find in this world—especially accompanied by the absolute love that fuels it. As you lay open my heart with your truth, help me not to run and hide; help me to trust your love enough to allow you to complete the "surgery" that will bring the health and well-being my soul longs for.

In God's Hands

Lord, I just want to tell you how much I love you, how grateful I am that you have taken me into your care. Ever since I've entrusted myself to you, you've kept me from becoming entangled in the kinds of things that would bring me to ruin. You fill my heart and mind with peace as I stay close to you. It's a miracle of your grace that I am standing tall tonight, lifting my praise to you from a heart full of love.

Behold, bless ye the Lord, all ye servants of the Lord, which by night stand in the house of the Lord. Lift up your hands in the sanctuary, and bless the Lord.

Psalm 134:1–2

Loving Others

O Lord, you are so serious about our loving one another that you even ask us to love our enemies. You are not satisfied if we merely pretend to love them either—you want us to genuinely love them! Such love demands more of us than we have to give, Lord. Only by drawing on the powerful love you offer will we be able to love all those around us. Stay with us always, Lord, and sustain our love for each other.

> But love ye your enemies, and do good,
> and lend, hoping for nothing again;
> and your reward shall be great,
> and ye shall be the children of the Highest.
>
> Luke 6:35

Return to Me

I remember hearing someone say once, "If God seems far away, guess who moved?" It's true, Lord: Sometimes I drift far away from you. I neglect reading your Word, I let my prayer life go by the wayside, and I get all tangled up in my attempts to handle everything on my own. I usually come to a sudden realization of how much I need you, and I am grateful for the epiphany! Even though I'm the one who's moved so far away, you don't hold it against me; you simply call me back.

God's Inspiration

Lord, thank you for being a part of my work today. I can always tell when a thought or an idea comes from you because it's just too perfect to have been my own! That you care enough to be involved in my work is a precious gift to me, Lord—one I would never want to be without.

The Lord recompense thy work, and a full reward be given thee of the Lord God of Israel, under whose wings thou art come to trust.

Ruth 2:12

Alleluia, Lord!

How we praise you with our words, our songs, and our lives! When we look back over all the situations you've brought us through, we are so grateful. We are filled with confidence that we can face the future because you will be there with us. And so we just want to stop today and praise you for all you are and all you do! Alleluia and Amen!

Let the people praise thee, O God;
let all the people praise thee.

Then shall the earth yield her increase;
and God, even our own God, shall bless us.

God shall bless us; and all the ends
of the earth shall fear him.

Psalm 67:5–7

False Gods

Lord, please keep me from falling into the trap of placing any other human on a pedestal. Even the most spiritual-seeming religious leaders are riddled with imperfection; they struggle with sin, just as I do. You alone are perfect and pure, and you alone are worthy of my adoration. I promise I will not follow anyone else, no matter how spiritually enlightened they may seem. There is no one like you, and you are the only one who will ever have my full devotion.

Through thy precepts I get understanding:
therefore I hate every false way.

Psalm 119:104

Accepting Forgiveness

O Lord, when you promise us you have removed our sins from us, why do we dredge them up so we can wallow in regret and shame all over again? Keep us from wasting time and energy thinking about past mistakes, Lord. If they are no longer on your radar, they surely don't belong on ours. How blessed we are to have such a compassionate, forgiving God!

> *To the Lord our God belong mercies and forgivenesses, though we have rebelled against him.*
>
> Daniel 9:9

Circles of Prayer

Tonight I thank you for those who pray for me, Father. Thank you for putting me in their hearts and minds. I know that at times today someone was keeping me in their prayers, and I hadn't the faintest clue. It could have been my hairdresser, chiropractor, pastor, or even someone I just met. Perhaps a checker at the grocery store recalled a bit of conversation we had and now prays for me from time to time. You work in such unusual ways that I never know how it might be happening—I just know that it is so, and I am grateful.

For the Lonely

Almighty God, tonight I pray for all those who feel love has passed them by. Due to the circumstances of their lives, they can't think of even one person who truly loves them. How hard it must be to reach out and love others if you have never felt the warmth of love yourself. How that could all change if they come to know you, God! Reach through the loneliness with your love, Father.

The Lord preserveth the strangers;
he relieveth the fatherless and widow.

Psalm 146:9

Resting in Your Love

Whenever I think of how you cherish me, I am amazed, Father. It's good for me to stop and remember that you actually delight in me, that you gave your most precious sacrifice to save me, and that there is nothing you would withhold from me that would benefit my life. I want to simply rest in the shade of your protective love right now as you impress your love on my heart.

My soul thirsteth for God, for the living God: when shall I come and appear before God?

Psalm 42:2

Countless Blessings

Lord, how good have you been to me? Let me count the ways! In times of discouragement all I need to do is sit quietly and remember all the times in the past when you stepped in to set wrongs right, gave me a second chance, or showed up with a last-minute miracle. Lord, you are so good. May my faith never waver in view of all the wonders you have wrought!

Blessed be the God and Father of our Lord
Jesus Christ, who hath blessed us with all
spiritual blessings in heavenly places in Christ.

Ephesians 1:3

Constant Growth

Lord, we are a people in search of a shortcut. Give us the five-minute dinner preparation and the instant credit. But we know, because you are so clear about this in your Word, that a mature faith can't be achieved overnight. Give us patience to endure, Lord. We are determined to become the complete individuals you intended us to be.

Shew me thy ways, O Lord; teach me thy paths.

Lead me in thy truth, and teach me:
for thou art the God of my salvation;
on thee do I wait all the day.

Remember, O Lord, thy tender mercies
and thy lovingkindnesses;
for they have been ever of old.

Psalm 25:4–6

My Sanctuary

Lord, when there seems to be no easy way out of a tough situation, I turn to you. When relationships seem too difficult to navigate, I turn to you. When I fear for my safety or feel threatened by bodily harm, I turn to you. You, O Lord, are my sanctuary. With you I am always safe. I praise you for this night and the day to follow!

He giveth power to the faint; and to them that have no might he increaseth strength.

Even the youths shall faint and be weary, and the young men shall utterly fall:

But they that wait upon the Lord shall renew their strength; they shall mount up with wings as eagles; they shall run, and not be weary; and they shall walk, and not faint.

Isaiah 40:29–31

My Stronghold and Refuge

Lord, we should not just turn to you in times of trouble, we should run to you. Where else can we find both shelter and consolation? Where else can we be both completely safe and unconditionally loved? Thank you for opening your arms to us whenever we need to run into them. Help us learn to run to you at the first sign of trouble. You are an unfailing refuge.

> Be merciful unto me, O God, be merciful unto me: for my soul trusteth in thee: yea, in the shadow of thy wings will I make my refuge, until these calamities be overpast.
>
> Psalm 57:1

After a Busy Day

O Lord, some days it seems that every hour is spent in toil, with little time left over for relaxing with loved ones. Help us keep in mind that our hours of work sow seeds of hope. In time, you will comfort us and restore us to a posture of joy and celebration. Thank you, Lord, for understanding both our need to work hard and our need to enjoy this beautiful life.

Blessed is every one that feareth the Lord; that walketh in his ways.

For thou shalt eat the labour of thine hands: happy shalt thou be, and it shall be well with thee.

Psalm 128:1–2

A Prayer of Trust

God, I know you're not in a hurry—
Your plans for me are on time.
You need no schedule or reminders
For I'm always on your mind.

I know you have drawn the mosaic
And You're fitting each tile in place.
As I continue to follow your plan,
Help me not to hurry or race.

Waiting is so often difficult,
And patience I don't easily learn.
But to have my life more Christ-like
Is for what I seek and yearn.

So as my life's pattern continues
And the next part begins to unfold,
It's you I'm trusting and praising,
It's your hand I cling to and hold.

Unceasing Prayer

Lord, if all the prayers ever prayed were linked together, surely they would reach to heaven and back countless times! We want to be a people who pray without ceasing, Lord. Hear both the prayers we utter and the silent prayers of our hearts, and may you also sense how grateful we are to serve a God who listens to our prayers and sends us his answers.

Rejoice evermore.

Pray without ceasing.

In every thing give thanks:
for this is the will of God in
Christ Jesus concerning you.

Quench not the Spirit.

1 Thessalonians 5:16–19

Self-Examination

The idea of an exam can strike fear into even the most prepared individuals. But the exam to which God's Word calls us is different from any dreaded math final or set of philosophical questions. This test is a self-checkup to see how we're doing—a chance to ask ourselves some probing questions and to answer them honestly. In the process, if we give ourselves some not-so-good marks, we don't need to beat ourselves up or become discouraged. Instead, we can use what we learn to initiate a fresh starting point for getting back into fellowship with our Lord.

A Difficult Situation

Lord, a vexing situation has me very confused. Is it possible I'm trying to sort it out through my own limited understanding and overlooking a crucial element? I know I can trust you with anything. I give this up to you and ask you to restore me to a place where I can look at what's going on in the right way—your way.

Then shalt thou understand the fear of the Lord, and find the knowledge of God.

For the Lord giveth wisdom: out of his mouth cometh knowledge and understanding.

He layeth up sound wisdom for the righteous: he is a buckler to them that walk uprightly.

Proverbs 2:5–7

Body and Spirit

Lord, sometimes I wonder what you think of this temple you created. There are some leaks in the roof and a few cracks in the walls. I have not always treated my body as a sacred temple for your Spirit. I've had days where I've felt deflated and I've found refuge in a few too many chocolates or a few too many sips of wine. Yet I know that even when I falter, your beautiful Spirit does not abandon ship! May I focus on that truth, Lord, and strive to be the being you want me to be.

Spiritual Hunger

*Y*ou truly do satisfy my spiritual hunger, Lord! In fact, when I'm away from you due to distractions or detours of my own making, I deeply feel the lack of you in my life. But then when I stop and take time to "feed" on your Word and spend time "drinking in" your comfort, I am strengthened and refreshed again. How true your Word is!

And Jesus said unto them, I am the bread of life: he that cometh to me shall never hunger; and he that believeth on me shall never thirst.

John 6:35

Like a River Glorious

Like a river glorious is God's perfect peace,

Over all victorious in its bright increase;

Perfect, yet it floweth fuller every day,

Perfect, yet it groweth deeper all the way.

Ev'ry joy or trial falleth from above,

Traced upon our dial by the sun of love;

We may trust him fuller all for us to do—

They who trust him wholly find him wholly true.

Stayed upon Jehovah, hearts are fully blest—

Finding, as he promised, perfect peace and rest.

Frances Ridley Havergal

PEACE

Dear God, tonight I long to feel the peace you bring, the peace that passes all under-standing. Fill my entire being with the light of your love, your grace, and your everlasting mercy. Be the soft place that I might fall upon to find the rest and renewal I seek.

Amen.

And let the peace of God rule in your hearts, to the which also ye are called in one body; and be ye thankful.

Let the word of Christ dwell in you richly in all wisdom; teaching and admonishing one another in psalms and hymns and spiritual songs, singing with grace in your hearts to the Lord.

Colossians 3:15–16

On a Winter Evening

Father God, the earth is asleep. The buds of spring lie in wait. The wonder of your world seems in a holding pattern just waiting for the go-ahead to grow. Let winter teach us the value of stillness, of silence, and of meditation. Help us know that the angel wings don't have to flutter wildly to do the work of your kingdom of peace.

The day is thine, the night also is thine: thou hast prepared the light and the sun.

Thou hast set all the borders of the earth: thou hast made summer and winter.

Psalm 74:16–17

Looking on the Night Sky

Creation shouts to me, Lord, about how amazing you are. I see the wonder of your wisdom in everything from the solar system to how bodies of water feed into one another to the life cycles of all living creatures. Everywhere I turn there is something that makes me think about how creative and insightful you are. Thank you for this universe that speaks without words. I hear it loud and clear, and it tells me of your magnificence.

> *And God saw every thing that he had made,*
> *and, behold, it was very good.*
>
> *Genesis 1:31*

Throughout the Generations

Lord, how grateful I am for the wise leaders

who came before me. Reading old journals,

books, and accounts of their lives, I see how

you were as active in their lives as you are in

ours today. Reading about the past gives us

hope and innovation for the future, and we

come away reassured that you are always

with us. Thank you, Lord, for your

steadfast love through all generations.

Time with the Lord

To grow in the grace of Christ is to embrace all that he freely offers me in the way of love, mercy, and salvation. And as I grow in his grace, I'll get better and better at extending love and mercy to others. To grow in the knowledge of Christ is to spend time with him in prayer and worship. As I spend more time with him, it will get easier and easier to follow the example he set for us.

As newborn babes, desire the sincere milk of the word, that ye may grow thereby:

If so be ye have tasted that the Lord is gracious.

1 Peter 2:2–3

Your People

The people I know who walk in the ways of God are savory with the fruit of God's Spirit; they're the kind of people I can't be around enough. Their kind and gentle ways radiate peace. Their joy is contagious. Their faithfulness is inspiring. So many things about them make me want to be more like them—and more like Christ.

The spirit be poured upon us from on high, and the wilderness be a fruitful field, and the fruitful field be counted for a forest.

Isaiah 32:15

Change My Heart

Father, you're always calling on us to turn our backs on sin and turn our faces toward you. You even promise to give us your own Spirit to lead and guide us and strengthen us to walk in your ways. I praise you tonight for your tireless love and concern for all people and for reaching out to us with your message of salvation.

*Turn us again, O Lord God of hosts, cause
thy face to shine; and we shall be saved.*

Psalm 80:19

Thy Will Be Done

O Lord, how wonderful are your promises! But because I trust your heart more than my own, I only want to receive the desires of my heart if they are desires that originate with you. Teach me to know the difference, Lord, between fleeting, worldly desires and those that have your blessing. Then, Lord—and only then—give me the desires of my heart. Amen.

Constant Thanks

Lord, how important it is for us to be thankful at all times. It's so easy to fall into the trap of having specific expectations and then despairing when events take an unexpected turn. You are working in our lives every moment, Lord. We will do our part by working hard and taking full advantage of all opportunities that come our way, but we also know that some matters are reserved for you. We are thankful that nothing is beyond your control, Lord, and we are grateful that you are our wise and loving leader.

The Big Picture

Sometimes it's good for me to just step back and look at the whole picture of who you are, Lord—to remember your greatness and meditate on all the implications of it. When I look at how big you are, my problems that seemed so gigantic a few moments ago suddenly seem almost silly. My big plans seem less important, and my high notions of myself get cut down to size. I come away not feeling diminished, though—rather lifted up in spirit and full of faith and gratitude. Surely we were made to praise you, Lord.

Your Peace

How restful it is to live in your love, Lord God! In the middle of chaos or turmoil, I remember that you are with me, and I am at peace once again. When it seems as if everything is falling apart, you hold me close in your love, and I am able to sleep at night. There is no other source of peace like belonging to you, Father.

Now the Lord of peace himself give
you peace always by all means.
The Lord be with you all.
2 Thessalonians 3:16

Boundless Generosity

Lord, you are the God who has set the foundations of the earth, who blessed Abraham with offspring "as numerous as the stars in heaven." You have blessed me, too, by giving me the treasure of my heart, my family. I pour out my thanks for these gifts, which are far above any riches the world can give. How can I praise you enough?

Heavenly Father, I never fail to come to you for help and comfort in the dark times of my life, yet I don't always remember you when my cup is overflowing. Forgive me if I seem ungrateful and take your generosity for granted. How can I forget all that you give me each day?

You bring beauty, peace, and love to my existence. My heart overflows with thanksgiving.

Seeking Your Wisdom

Lord, so often I believe I know exactly what I think and why, but then I sense your gentle nudging to look at the situation from your perspective. How generous of you to shine your wisdom into the dark corners of my heart and mind! Make me a believer wise in your ways—not one determined to have things my own way.

O the depth of the riches both of the wisdom and knowledge of God! how unsearchable are his judgments, and his ways past finding out!

Romans 11:33

Waiting for Your Answer

$\mathcal{I}$ confess, Lord, that in my haste to come to you in prayer and to present my laundry list of requests, I forget the other side of prayer. I forget to listen for your answer. I know that if I am patient enough, your gentle message will come to me when I wait for it.

Forgive me my impatience, Father, when I ask for your help with my problems, then fail to listen to your response. Thank you for teaching me that if I seek, I will find. Help me to seek and listen for your answers, written across the pages of my heart.

Your Awesome Creation

How do I explain to my children your greatness, O God? How do I tell of all your wonderful works? I will tell them to look up. The sky displays the work of your hands.

By day, in blazing splendor, the sun bespeaks your power. In the inverted black bowl of night, the stars shout your glory. Orion, Pleiades, the Bear, make their seasonal journey across the wide expanse in praise of you. Even the moon reflects your wondrous light.

The sky says it all, O Lord. We just need to look up to see what you have done.

A Community of Believers

Lord, my heart is uplifted as I think of the special gift you have given me: a community of faith. I thank you for my church and for the dear people who have become part of my support system. I thank you for your invitation to spend time with you.

My spouse and children and I need the blessings of church attendance. We need the fellowship and care of other believers; we need to be refreshed with the words of Scripture and feel the power of prayer washing over us. We need to experience your presence, Lord, in your house, and to become involved in your work.

Please continue to strengthen our children's ties to your church so that they, too, may participate in the joys of life in the Christian community.

Hearing Your Word

How we love a good story, O Divine Love. Especially a story with hope and promise and a good ending. When it comes to your Book, give me an open ear so that I might hear your good news, an open mind ready to accept it, and an open heart willing to be transformed by your love and acceptance of me.

I had gone with the multitude, I went with them to the house of God, with the voice of joy and praise, with a multitude that kept holyday.

Psalm 42:4

Giving God Control

I know that releasing control to you, Lord, is one of the hardest but most rewarding steps of obedience that I will ever take. Trusting in your faithfulness and submitting to your authority may seem like leaping headfirst into a river; I feel safe standing on the shoreline, looking at the roaring waves below, but I know I'm missing out on your best plans for my life. Yes, jumping into the river will sweep me away to places unknown—and it will take all of my strength and effort to navigate the waters—but the adventure will be so worth it!

I want to trust in your faithfulness. I believe that you have great things in store for me. You won't lead me down a river only to abandon me or leave me injured on the riverbed. My soul is precious to you, and you have a purpose in mind for my life. You are faithful, and I will claim that truth as I jump headfirst toward my destiny.

In Times of Weakness

*Y*ou give your help, O Comforting God, not in proportion to our merit, but based only on our need. For you come not only to those who are "keeping it together," but to those of us who are fragmented and fractured. I need the tenderness of your caress so that I know I am not alone in my awful feelings of weakness.

A Parent's Prayer

Over and over I ask myself, O Loving Shepherd, "What can I do?" What can I do to help, to make a difference, to relieve those I love of their hurts? The hardest thing about this parenting role is having others think I can "fix it" and then finding out that I can't, as much as I would like to. Remind me that what you promise is not to "fix it" for us but rather to give us whatever it takes to prevail in spite of our hurts. Help me to see that sharing a tear is sometimes all that is necessary.

Teaching Children to Pray

Father in heaven, we want to teach our children how to pray. We want them to greet you in the morning, to thank you at meals, to reflect and rest in your presence at night. There are so many things we want them to know about prayer, but where do we start? How do we explain that though you always hear us, your answer may not come right away? How do we get them beyond the recitation of rote prayers to express prayers from their hearts? How do we discourage frivolous prayers without stifling spontaneity?

It is an awesome thing, Lord, to instruct our children in your ways. Guide us as we teach them about the most important conversations they will ever have.

Building Up Faith

Faith and fear cannot coexist. One always gives way to the other. It is necessary for us to be constantly building up our faith to overcome all the sources of destructive disbelief all around us. We need to be continually working at rekindling the gift of God that is in us, which is our faith in him and in his promises. We must be dedicated to developing a spirit of love and power and discipline within ourselves. Studying the words of the holy scriptures, meditating on them, keeping God's commandments, and praying daily are some of the ways we can keep our faith strong. By focusing on these things, we shut out fear and cultivate faith.

Comfort After a Long Day

Like aching bones that find relief in a steamy,

hot bath, O God, that's the comfort I long for.

Take from my life the fear, the hurt, the doubt,

the unknown, the insecurity—the afflictions.

Nonetheless, your promise is to comfort us in

our afflictions not remove them. Help me to

know that I will experience the "relief"

I want only when I am open to accepting

your healing comfort that gives us the

strength to triumph.

In Memory

Lord, you have told us to "remember the days of old." Memorials have played a large part in the history of your people in Israel, and we thank you for these reminders to honor the past.

As we remember those who have gone before us, we teach our children love and respect for life itself.

In giving honor to others, we thank and honor you, O God, for your love and for the great sacrifice of your son, Jesus Christ.

Placing My Faith in You

When the winds of change and challenge blow hard into my life, I will take refuge in you, O Lord. When the darkness descends upon my house and home, I will fear not for I will place my faith in you, O Lord. When my child is ill or my spouse is hurt, I will remain steadfast, for I know that you will be right there by my side, O Lord. Although I cannot see you, I know you are always with me, O Lord, and in that I take comfort and find strength.

Getting the Children to Bed

Lord, why is it that when I am the most tired or crave sleep myself, the children's bedtime becomes prolonged and difficult? There is always one last drink of water, one final trip to the bathroom, one more bedtime story, or one more postscript to the prayer. By then, desperation sets in, and my temper becomes short.

God of peace, help me to face bedtime more calmly. Help me to discover strategies for helping my children to wind down and relax. Prevent me from losing my temper, and grant me a soothing manner so the children's last memories of the day are pleasant and loving. Thank you, Lord, for your promise of a safe and peaceful sleep.

Staying Up Late

O God of rest and rejuvenation, guide me to find ways to let your nurturing reach me. I need to be healthy and well-rested in order to provide, lead, and inspire. Burning the candle at both ends all the time is hardly an example I'm proud of.

And on the seventh day God ended his work which he had made; and he rested on the seventh day from all his work which he had made.

Genesis 2:2

In Thanksgiving for Good Neighbors

Lord, if only everyone could adopt your law of love as our neighbors have. I thank you for sending us good friends who are always ready to give our children shelter and a cookie in any emergency, to lend equipment or advice, to offer an occasional ride or a meal—to help out in any way they can. Where would we be without their valued assistance and generosity?

I am grateful for their kindness, their willingness, and their generous spirits. Bless these loving people, Father, who are your hands reaching out to care for us.

Please make me a good neighbor to them, and may I find many opportunities to return your love by helping them when they are in need.

Friendship in the Lord

*G*od, a call, a note, and a handclasp from a friend are simple and seemingly insignificant. Yet you inspire these gifts from people we have a special affection for. These cherished acts of friendship nudge aside doubts about who we are when we feel low and encourage our hearts in a way that lifts our spirits. Thank you for the friends you have given us.

A man that hath friends must shew himself friendly: and there is a friend that sticketh closer than a brother.

Proverbs 18:24

In Times of Strife

It is so easy to become overwhelmed, O faithful Spirit, by the needs surrounding us. Our voices join with the faithful through the centuries who have pleaded for the coming of your kingdom, for an end to the violence and suffering. We have prayed for restitution and justice to overcome deceit and despair. Give us strength to continue to do our part, courage to stand apart, and compassion to reach out to those who have been torn apart by their life experiences. Help us change the world with you, one moment at a time.

Whatever tests in life you're facing, whether it's a challenge of relationships, finances, or your career, the loving Spirit that created you is always available to guide you into a better life.

Past, Present, and Future

The past, O God of yesterdays, todays, and promise-filled tomorrows, can be an anchor or a launching pad. It's sometimes so easy to look back on the pain and hurt and believe the future may be an instant replay. Help us to accept the aches of the past and put them in perspective so we can also see the many ways you supported and nurtured us. Then, believing in your promise of regeneration, launch us into the future free and excited to live in joy.

Hope in the Lord

As I trust in you, God, I know you will fill my life with your hope. That hope will transcend into every area of my soul, and beautiful buds of joy and peace will begin to grow. I want your joy and peace to be obvious in my life.

I'm tired of pretending to be joyful and acting like I'm peaceful. I desire those fruits to grow naturally, out of the wellspring of hope in my heart.

Prod me to trust you at all times, Lord, and to rely on your Word. I know that my joy and peace are complete in you, and I have hope that you can work in me despite my weaknesses.

I'm done with putting my hope into the changing tides of this world. I'm ready to put all of my hope in you, so real fruits of joy and peace can grow.

A Meditation on Hope

Hope is an anchor to the soul. It can keep us from drifting aimlessly, getting caught in whirlpools, or running into sandbars. This anchor is essential in a world so full of various waves. Sometimes those waves slap us from behind; sometimes we see them coming but cannot get out of the way. In all cases, hope ties us to safety. The waves come and go in their fury or playfulness—but hope is always there.

Worry

Lord, sometimes I worry about my loved ones. Though I often complain of the monotony of my day-to-day life, I know my days are full of moments to be treasured. When I hear shocking, horrific stories on the news, I often wonder how I would handle such events if they were to befall me or a loved one. Father, I cling to your promise that you give each of us a future filled with hope. I am grateful that you hear me when I come to you in prayer. Please stay close to me and my loved ones. Grant us the strength to prevail in all circumstances.

God's Choice

Dear God, isn't it funny how much better I feel when I choose to love? And yet how many times in the course of my life have I chosen anger or hatred or fear? Let me always choose love first, for when I do make that choice, it opens up the doorway to new friendships and joy that other choices cannot give me. Make love be not only my first choice but my only choice. Thank you, God, for choosing to love me.

True Security

God, I feel happy tonight, and I have you to thank for that. No matter what is going on outside of me, I am strong and safe and secure inside because you love and care for me. Thank you for loving me when I have been cranky, tired, lazy, and even mean. Thank you for being there when I ignored your presence, God. Your steadfast love is a constant reminder of just how good I have it in life. And that makes me happiest of all!

God's Renewal

God, when I am tired and just feeling down about everything in my life, your love reminds me that there is a spring of hope and renewal I can drink from anytime. It may take me awhile to come around, but I always come back to love as the reason to keep on going, even when my gas tank is empty. Love fuels me and makes me ready for whatever new challenge you have in store for me tomorrow.

Call to Action

We know, Lord, that action is the proper fruit of knowledge and all spiritual insight. But so often we wish only to think and muse, without ever doing good toward anyone.

Yes, it's easier to know the good than to do it. It's more comforting to be right than to do the right thing. It's more convenient to sit on the sidelines and give advice than it is to enter the game. It takes less energy to tell others how to carry their burdens than to take up a share of the load with them. But we need to be shaken out of our lethargy, God. We need to recognize that our lack of love is evident in our lack of good deeds. We need to see ourselves, so often, just as we are: sometimes selfish, often lazy.

Change us, God! Let these reflections tonight inform our actions tomorrow. Open our eyes that we may see the needs around us. Show us the poor— and all the ways we can help. Bring us to the sick— giving us words of comfort and creative means of succor. Let us no longer pass by the hungry stranger, but move us to offer what is in our hand and in our cupboard to share.

Help us to take the more difficult route of service. Help us to forsake the ease and comfort of a purposeless life. Help us to make friends with the unlikable, to bond with those who are different. Help us to take all we know and put it into every resource at hand, so that action may result for the good of all.

For if you will show us that we, too, are poor and hungry, feeble and needy in so many ways, then we will recognize that our giving can only spring from what we have already been given.

Evening Prayer

Watch, dear Lord, with those who wake,

or watch, or weep tonight,

and give your angels charge over those

who sleep.

Tend your sick ones, O Lord Christ,

Rest your weary ones.

Bless your dying ones.

Soothe your suffering ones.

Pity your afflicted ones.

Shield your joyous ones.

And all for your love's sake.

Amen.

St. Augustine